Prayers AND PIECES

Paula J. Reeder

ISBN 979-8-89243-752-3 (paperback)
ISBN 979-8-89243-753-0 (digital)

Christian Faith Publishing
832 Park Avenue
Meadville, PA 16335
www.christianfaithpublishing.com

Printed in the United States of America

CONTENTS

ACKNOWLEDGMENTS

I have to give a heap of thanks to the many elders whom I love and adore, one of whom is my sister Dawn Miller. I'll never forget the day we all piled into her car for church, and someone asked, "Do we have to listen to this kind of music?" (It was a Christian radio station.)

She quickly replied, "My car, my music." I'd say that was a gentle witness. Kristina Cranston was an amazing elder as well.

Marilyn Bolen, Alex Hirzel, Candy Bazil, and Carol Goliatowski were the "usual suspects," as well as an amazing deacon named Maria Girardi, who always "showed up" when presentation was key. These women live with their hearts for Christ. Thank you for your willingness, faithfulness, and friendship.

I had to laugh. When my brother and I were very young, we snuck into the communion room at our church. Our mother was busy giving piano lessons, and we were impatient and *starving* for lunch. My brother knew which cupboard held all the goodness, and we grabbed a handful of each of the communion wafers and shoved them in our mouths, crunching them in delight. I suddenly thought to ask him, "Won't we get in trouble for eating these?"

He very simply replied, "Well, David did it in the Bible and didn't get in trouble, so we can too! It will be okay!" So we helped ourselves to a glass of Welch's grape juice too! That was for the wine for the service, of course. When the piano lesson was over, we started feeling a bit guilty. Mom can always tell when something's up. One of the deaconesses came in to prepare the communion as we were leaving. She asked my mom if anyone had been in the supplies. Of course, we confessed. When my mother heard our reasoning, she had to quietly chuckle but be stern and remind us of the elements being holy and that they're not just grape juice and bread. She also said, "Yes, all are welcome at God's table, but it's a special time to understand his grace and mercy." She finally just laughed and extended that grace and mercy to us as well. We did, however, have to apologize and promise not to do it again.

CHAPTER 1

Two Minutes at God's Table

1. "We gather at your table, Lord, with our hearts contrite,
   Remembering you gathered with your friends, on the left and
       right,
   The bread your body, the cup your blood, the gifts they both
       entail,
   Your love so rich flowing down, both hands pierced by nails,
   We thank you, Lord." Amen.

2. "We are all equal at your table, all sinners falling short,
   All saved by grace, a little or a lot, just giving you our hearts,
   The bread your body, the cup your blood,
   Our sins upon your cross,
   Eternally we'll be with you, you wanted no one lost."

3. "We come to your table hungry,
   Hungry for grace, the bread your body,
   Hungry for mercy, the cup your crimson blood,
   Fill us with forgiveness and guide us.
   We are all broken, some in shards.
   Fill us with your Holy Spirit whole and new."

4.   "Resting at your table, Lord, worn by world affairs,
Glad that we can make the time, like that night upstairs,
Best friends gathered, one not so true yet invited all the same,
'The bread, take, eat, this is my body,' Master, please explain,
'The cup, drink, this is my blood, do this in remembrance of me'
Master, we don't understand but we do all agree,
Years later we understand, the disciples all took part,
You made a way, for you to be, forever in our hearts."

5.   "King of kings and Lord of lords, humble as a man,
Sacrificed upon the cross, a special pure white lamb,
Bread and wine, body and blood, we celebrate your grace,
We hold these gifts in our hearts, until we see your face."

6.   "Holding hands around your table, candles lit in the presence of
     your Spirit,
Serving each other the bread your body, the cup your blood,
May your love pass through hands held,
May our hearts be lifted knowing that grace and mercy abounds."

7.   "Breaking bread at your table, drinking wine, its power healing,
Grace abounds where it's needed, thankful, grateful hearts are
     seated,
Heads are bowed we all remember, your sacrifice, our hearts to
     render." Amen.

8.   "The upper room, our homes, your table, anywhere we share in
     Spirit,
Bread, biscuit, it's all one, juice, wine, we all take some,
In celebration of your love, in celebration of new life in you." Amen.

9.   "You prayed in the garden alone, 'Father, thy will be done,'
You hung on a wooden cross, 'Father, forgive them for they
     know not what they do,'
The gift of love, the gift of grace you've given us,
This bread, this cup, may our hearts remember." Amen.

10. "Table blessings, bread and cup, the lovely lamb Christ, now we sup,
All together, Spirit one, Lord, may thy work be done." Amen.

11. "Oh Lord, you defeated death, you defeated the evil one,
You gave your body, our bread; you gave your blood, our cup;
we thank you, Lord." Amen.

12. "We gather at your table, Lord, your Son on our minds,
As he died upon the cross, his blood flowed down, the wine,
The bread his body, a gift of love, grace it just abounds,
May we share your sacrifice to those we are around." Amen.

13. "Father of all creation, speak to us for we gather to hear you,
Whisper our names for we are your children,
As we pour this cup, may we remember,
As all of us break bread together, speak to our hearts." Amen.

14. "You carried a cross upon your back, they pierced your hands
with nails,
A crown of thorns upon your head, so that everyone may live,
This bread your body, this cup your blood, your suffering our
gift,
Your resurrection our gift, we thank you." Amen.

15. "May this quiet time of reflection on your sacrifice bring to
mind the gifts of love you gave." Amen.

16. "Oh Savior, we celebrate new life in you, these elements, your
gifts are true,
Oh Savior, we love you." Amen.

17. "Heavenly Father,
"We gather at your table, Lord, no longer slaves to sin,
For by your grace the bread your body, new life in us begins,
Mercy flowing, a crimson cup, your blood it does abound,

No longer bound by chains of guilt, no shame will there be
    found,
Held in your arms embraced by love, we hold this in our hearts,
Your Holy Spirit now surrounds us as we all take part." In your
    holy name, amen.

This prayer is dedicated to my grandmother, Ethel Keen.

This was one of my prayers and blessings for a grandma who was *puppy-sitting* while I blessed the young couple's home, who were the parents of the puppy. I stopped by to see how she fared. I had to laugh as it "piddled" on the carpet and then dragged her slipper, while she screamed the puppy's name, chasing it under the bed. It finally came out, sorry and remorseful, and she scooped it up in her arms. It kissed her chin, and she melted and kissed it back.

I was on my way to a very important doctor's appointment, trying to merge onto the highway. A shiny black sedan came racing up the right lane just as I was about to merge, causing me to brake, and then he cut over to the speed lane on the left to get around the middle lane. I yelled, "Can't you see I was trying to merge?" But then I quickly thought, *Maybe there's a baby on the way, or maybe someone's sick, or who knows.* Only God. So perhaps it'd just be best to say a prayer, still my heart, and be thankful no one was hurt.

CHAPTER 2

Blessings

1. Lord,

This young couple's home is fresh and new, like a canvas awaiting paint.

May your Holy Spirit guide them in creating a wonderful canvas of memories and pictures. May they lead in love, your love, Lord, and remember to share time together with you. A home shared with you first is already blessed in love.

2. Lord,

This family has a wonderful new addition to their family. Black and furry, white or gray, brown or mixed, four paws or feathers, they are your creations. Angels in disguise? Or perhaps just for humor, hugs, affection, life lessons, and many other reasons. They do mostly teach us discipline and how to care for other living creatures. May you lay a hand of peace and guidance on this family and their beloved pet for the years they get to enjoy each other.

3. Lord,

Bless this driver in a hurry, no signals, speeding, breaking laws. Whatever's causing them to do this, Lord, we know you know the cause. Ease our hearts and keep us safe.

So my brother and I are only one year apart. My next-to-oldest brother was studying the German language, and I loved to lay on the warm church floor tiles and listen to his German records while he buffed the floors. We were the custodians. So Sunday came, and they grouped the first and second graders in the same classroom to save on teachers.

Our teacher, Mrs. Duncan, put us in a circle and asked if we had anything that we would like to share with the class. I quickly raised my hand and said I would like to sing "Jesus Loves Me" in German! My younger brother had a perplexed look on his face like, "Oh no, here we go," but remained silent.

So Mrs. Duncan looked quite surprised and said, "Go ahead, Paula!"

So taking a deep breath and thinking in my head, *Okay Paula, every word has to end in ein,* I proceeded to sing to the tune of "Jesus Loves Me." "*Ein blein stein klein blein einstein, ein blein stein blein einstein klein, blein einstein blein stein einstein, blein stein einstein blein klein blein.*" Then "Yes, Jesus loves me…and so on…"

Everyone clapped, and my younger brother looked completely horrified. Mrs. Duncan raised her white handkerchief to her mouth in an attempt to hide her laughter, but her shaking shoulders and dabs at her tearing eyes gave her away. I thought perhaps she was moved. She then, after composing herself, said, "Thank you, Paula. I'm sure you meant to sing that in German, but I'm sure some of those words weren't quite right." I was once again extended grace that only a seasoned Sunday school teacher, an amazing group of friends, a loving older brother, and Christ would give, whom I'm sure may have chuckled too, knowing that he was loved by a group of children and a teacher that day.

CHAPTER 3

Offerings

1. Jehovah Jireh,
   Giver of all good gifts, we thank you,
   Giver of all good gifts, we bless you,
   Giver of all good gifts, we return to you,
   lay upon our hearts how to use these for your kingdom.

2. We are your sons and daughters, you care for us as a good parent.
   All our needs are met physically, spiritually, financially, and for
   our best interest or our best walk.
   We may not understand our journeys, but we know you are with
   us.
   May those struggling financially with needs have their needs
   met.
   We return to you these gifts. May they be blessed.

3. We experience peaks and valleys in our walks with you as we
   learn and grow.
   Financially as well. We return to you as you lay upon our hearts
   what is required of each of us.
   May this be multiplied for your kingdom.

4. Each new day brings a new beginning. Each new day brings
   a new experience. What a wonderful gift to spend a day with

you, Lord. We celebrate the many gifts you give us. We return these gifts to you in many ways. We return these gifts as money, hugs, rides, meals, and smiles; you alone know how these gifts are returned sometimes. May they all be used for your glory. Keep our hearts contrite in doing so.

5. We thank you for the gift of life. We thank you for the gift of life in you. We thank you for our material gifts, for we need them to live. May we remember to always return to you our firstfruits.

Our portions to you come first. You alone know our hearts. Guide us with your Holy Spirit. May those in need have their needs met and have a permanent financial solution through you. Teach us, O Lord, thy ways that we may be able to teach others. May we always be good examples.

6. You clothed the birds of the air and the flowers of the fields, and yet we worry. Lord, we come to you in prayer. We give you our offerings. May these offerings be multiplied for your glorification and your kingdom.

7. More than just the things you give us, we thank you for the things to come. The new beginnings, new arrivals, newness in you of those we love. We return to you our tithes and love in ways you've laid upon our hearts. May we always be good listeners.
In your glorious name,

8. Lord, you are so very generous. We all have eaten; we all have met our due. We now return to you what we have set aside for you. Bless the first fruit of the blessings you've given us. May it be used for your kingdom.
In your holy name,

9. As we contemplate our givings, may each of us remember what we are thankful for. May we give you all praise. For it is from you

that we receive all gifts, and to you now we return these gifts, for your work.

I don't remember whose idea it was to do a foot washing. The pastor and I agreed that we'd be the foot washers during the service. We prayed before the service in his office with the deacon.

I remember the feeling of humbleness and servitude. It was a feeling of complete grace, washing everyone's feet. There were the feet of a person in front of me, someone who had humiliated and challenged me. I didn't mind washing their feet. As I applied scented oil, I hoped that somehow in their heart there was a spark of kindness, or perhaps a chance for change, where the Holy Spirit could move. And *by golly*, it happened in mine. It bothered me that this person never softened, but I prayed for them daily and still do.

I suppose Jesus calmly sat at the table with Judas at the Last Supper, knowing the betrayal was coming.

I suppose Jesus calmly drew the line in the sand when confronted with stones ready to throw.

I suppose Jesus calmly steadied the sea and took Peter's hand.

And I suppose we of little faith sometimes best be calm when faced with the things we think God can't handle.

CHAPTER 4

The Gatherings

1. Early we gather, singing praises, lifting your name, lifting our
       hands,
   Each voice raises, "Forgive us, Lord," each voice raises, "Hear
       us, Lord."
   Different races, different walks, the Holy Spirit gathers its flock,
   Guide us gently with advice, from the Shepherd, Father God,
   We, your sons and daughters, now rejoice.

2. Horns blowing, drums pounding, cymbals crashing, hands clap-
   ping, voices raising, all in unison, one accord, a joyful noise unto
   our lord. Everyone happy in one Spirit. Yours, Lord.

3. Fire embers glowing, blankets on the ground, a soft guitar
   strumming, kids sitting around. Two leaders standing, loading
   s'mores on crooked wooden sticks. Giggles, gales of laughter, all
   the while the Holy Spirit amidst.

4. Walking, marching arm in arm as one body, singing, praying,
       "Lord, we are your army.
   Give us your grace and your mercy, may we do your will,
   Ease our embers, flames of fury, guide us with your bridle,
   Move us with your Holy Spirit, may we speak your words,

Lay your wisdom on the issues, peace upon our hearts,
May our lives begin again, each with a new start."

5. We climbed a mountain to get close to you yet found we were
        closer on the ground.
    Sure-footed, without a clear view of the path, we found our faith
        abound.
    On top of the mountain, we saw the path but almost fell with
        our own view.
    Funny how things go sometimes when we don't put our trust
        in you.

6. Lying on the grass, I marveled at your art. Oh Lord, Creator of
        all things, how great thou really art.
    Each blade of grass, perfectly made, different but the same,
    Each like people, thousands, millions, different colors, blends,
        or shades,
    Each with a different purpose, but the same.

7. We worship thee, oh King! On a donkey's back, palm leaves
    spread, and praises raised while cheers well said! All the while
    with gloom awaiting and a tomb.

8. Waving branches left and right, the disciples lined the path with
        fright,
    Not understanding the path of Christ, they watched in wonder
        for Pharisees or plight.
    The people cheered, but Jesus knew, all along what he would do,
    In the garden, alone he prayed, "Father, can you take this cup away?"
    "Thy will be done, it's your will, not mine," Judas made sure an
        army to find,
    Several disciples slept, and Jesus wept, Jesus his promise to God
        was kept.
    Peter defended with his sword, but Jesus said, "No!" I'll wear
        their cords,

Led away tied and bound, while John ran fast not to be found,
"Mary, they took him. Come quick!" John said, and then the
gatherings, Christ's judgment began.

I was preparing the sanctuary for a Good Friday service, and I had to hang a crown of thorns on our hand-hewn rugged cross. Placing my hand on the cross, I carefully balanced the crown on a pole with my other hand and began the tricky catch of hooking it on the nail on the crossbeam.

It almost caught, but…alas! It fell off the hook, and in an automatic reflex, I stuck my safe hand out to catch it. Oh, the thorn that pierced the meat of my thumb seared with a pain that burned as it tore the flesh. As blood quickly dripped, I dropped everything and ran to the restroom, turned on the faucet, and watched the blood flow down the drain, all the while thinking…

Oh, Lord, they crammed a crown of these thorns on your head and tore your flesh. Your blood mingled with sweat and tears ran into your eyes, stinging, and you couldn't move for you were bound. Beaten, your clothing stripped from you, and they left you naked and jeered.

I quickly bandaged my hand and realized I had been crying. Quietly. The weight of our sins, shame, guilt, and pain, accusations, and yet he said, "Father, forgive them, for they know not what they do."

My scar has since faded from my thumb. Our Savior's scars have never faded. Such grace and mercy are the same today as they were then.

CHAPTER 5

Just You and Me, God

1. Sitting at the water's edge, just as a grain of sand,
   So many people in this world, God, do you understand?
   You hear our prayers all at once, yet you hold me in your hand,
   Strong and gentle, safe and sure, I'll follow your command.

2. No one here but you and me, and I'm angry as a bee.
   God, you said, "I'll be here," just you follow me.
   Where were you when I got hurt, and I lost my job and fell?
   I lost my car, Lord, everything, I may, oh, just as well…
   I'm going to sit here angry, Lord, and wait for your reply,
   See, no one else will have me now, not me, myself, nor I.
   So I guess I came on pretty rough, I'm sorry, please forgive,
   And show me in this silent space, exactly how I'll live.
   If you're silent now, I'll understand, I didn't mean to yell,
   I'm sure you have some type of plan, that only time can tell.

3. Oh Lord, the lake is beautiful, the breeze is on my face,
   Only you could create this quiet kind of space.
   Your Holy Spirit at my heart, all grievances let go,
   I feel the coolness fill my body from my head to my toes.
   No noise, just peace, this special place, we have to share within,
   To ground me for the week ahead, the busy grinding din.

So thank you, Lord, for all your care and all that's up above, your
    gentleness
That fills my heart, the peace of a white dove.

4.   Lord, I know you see my son, the way he lives and acts,
I ask your patience and protect him, 'til he turns 'round back.
A difficult predicament he's in, for sure, as a child he gave you
    his heart,
He never quite then matured, got lost, and fell apart.
I'm asking, Lord, a mother's prayer, his journey comes full sway,
Like Joseph and his coat of colors, or Daniel, or Jonah, eh?
Perhaps he'll have a testimony full of stories abroad, to lead his
    brothers, sisters, others, many back to God.

5.   There is a man that I know, he is my father-in-law,
Through the years of knowing him, several things I saw,
How he loves his family dearly, always puts others first,
How he lent a helping hand when things were at their worst.
Please, Lord, there is one thing that I would really wish,
That in your heavenly realm he and his wife have eternal bliss.

6.   Lord, I'm in the car again, just to get away, driving down the
    highway just to scream and then to pray.
As tears flow down, I feel your touch, the sunbeam on my cheek,
All at once, our talk begins, and peace fills the seat.
We pick a song on the radio, then drive into the night,
Talking all the while, and remembering what's right.
A verse, a proverb, it all makes sense, get gas, then go back home,
No one knows about our talks, dinner is ready, rrrrrrring…the
    phone.

7.   I lit a candle, finding time, an hour just to spare, try to be inten-
    tional, but Lord, it's just not there.
Pick up kids, go to work, today is all I got, so is one hour a week
    okay? It is an easy spot.
No one is home, it's just our time, I'm coming to you in prayer,

Just to listen, just to sing, I don't have much to share.
So please forgive me if I'm plain, not fancy talking stuff,
May our tiny one hour a week be just enough.

8. Jesus, sometimes I wonder what your childhood was like. Did
    you skin your knees?

    Did you play fun games or eat silly food and serious food too?
    Even though I know the sacredness of baptism and being one
    with you, did you ever just get to swim too?

    Every time I do everything, I marvel and see you in it. Should I?
    I cupped water in my hands while standing in a lake and thought
    about all the wonderful things it creates. Then I remembered,
    you created water. Thank you.

9. Lord, I'm gardening today. I'm turning the earth upside down
    and smelling the rich brown soil underneath and crumbling the
    clods in my hands. Every stone I touch reminds me of David
    and Goliath. I set them aside for my son's collection. Every big
    worm I remember serves a purpose. I remember the parable of
    the sower and the seeds, and I'm careful to make a perfect hole
    and drop the seed in, carefully covering it. Carefully watering
    the seed, I then wait to see what grows. Patience, God, you must
    have great patience to watch us grow. Thank you, God.

10. Oh Lord, the first time I saw the ocean and the skyline, I had to
    pull my car over and cry.

    Your omnipresence is huge! Only you could create such beauty
    and vastness. To look to where there is no end and realize how
    far the east is from the west is breathtaking. I looked up into the
    night sky into the eternity of stars and saw no end as well. How
    many galaxies, how many moons? I then realize the magnitude
    of your forgiveness and the depth of your mercy and grace.

11. Oh heavenly Father,

I marveled at the intricate body you gave me. Each cell, each muscle, organ, nerve, or valve, everything performing a function.

Its perfect timing all in accord, allowing us to play different roles, even with minor defects or handicaps or injuries, our bodies can constitute and play a part in our walks.

Very humbling, very necessary in your greatest plan of all. We thank you.

12. Oh, Holy Father,

God, I fear you. I tremble at your holy name. That day in the sanctuary, when we were alone, I yelled and screamed and sang at you in frustration and in fear. Yet you calmly sent your Holy Spirit through the windows in a sunbeam, wrapping its arms around me.

I sat on the pew for just a few more moments and felt the warmth of your love on the back of my neck. The fire of your Holy Spirit slowly entering my now repentant heart and the sweet rest that now fills my soul. Tasks are slowly lying in place that I must accomplish to apologize or set things right with those I hurt. I didn't know how off track I was until I talked it out with you, God. I was afraid to be wrong. I felt justified. I know now. Thank you, Holy Father.

No Pride Allowed

13. I banged the piano in a chord not often heard. Others heard me, turning their heads murmuring, "She's talented." My pride grew like a monster in the sanctuary of my heart, never letting others hear the display of chords for fear of rejection. See, I used that piano to release the secret grief and anger that God and I

shared, and no one else. But, somehow, it wasn't enough to keep it to myself. So I played the chords in anguish in private, or when others heard, or whenever I could, and when others asked, "Why don't you share this gift?" I'd make up answers, and then I'd offer to sing or find some other way to dodge the bullet of "I only play by ear and fear."

CHAPTER 6

Passing to Heaven

1. Dear Lord,

    Your son is soon to meet you in heaven. He believes with all his heart you are the Christ, the Son of the Living God, and that you died for his sins. I'm holding his hand so that he knows he's not alone on this earth. Please hold him now with your Holy Spirit and reassure him that when he closes his eyes to rest, he will be with you and those saints who have passed before him. We love you, Lord. In your glorious name,

2. Dear Lord,
    Thank you for angels all around us, making sure the path is clear,
    Making sure this sister, brother never even shed a tear.
    Forever now they have a room, in a mansion, no more gloom,
    No pain, no suffering, just a gate, where they meet you and
        celebrate.

3. Dear Jesus,
    I watched a dove land on the ground; it walked left and then right,
    Looking at my face, its wings stretched out, then took flight.
    It hovered just a bit, then landed on my hand.
    At first, I was a bit afraid, but now I understand,

Like Peter on the water, or Jonah in the whale,
Lord, you use mysterious ways to reach us when we're frail.
Dying's just another path, another step of faith,
And when we finally do let go, we'll see your glorious face.

ABOUT THE AUTHOR

I grew up as the youngest of six children, with one mother cleaning a church. My mother was the organist as well. We had many adventures growing up and delving into the faith. This book includes parts of my childhood, graced with simplicity. As an elder, it reminds me to pray with the simplicity of that grace given and, when necessary, to extend grace to those we pray with or for. After all, if it wasn't for grace, we'd all be in trouble. I attended Kentucky Wesleyan College and have published poetry through the International Library. I also dabble in photography, with several published photos in Silent Spark Press and Nature Conservancy. I won't accept profit for my writings, as the proceeds will be used in a ministry creating churches, farming, and schools or hospitals in Mozambique, so they may know the love of Christ and his grace. My grandmother loved children, and I do as well. She inspired me to write, mostly so I'd be quiet during her two TV shows and laughed as I interrupted her anyway. Enjoy this book. Keep prayers simple.